AN AMERICAN EDUCATION AGENDA

Top 15 Recommendations For Improving K-12 Education

LANCE IZUMI

An American Education Agenda
Top 15 Recommendations for Improving K-12 Education
by Lance Izumi, J.D.

December 2017

ISBN: 978-1-934276-36-5

Pacific Research Institute
101 Montgomery Street, Suite 1300
San Francisco, CA 94104
Tel: 415-989-0833
Fax: 415-989-2411
www.pacificresearch.org

Download copies of this study at www.pacificresearch.org.

Nothing contained in this report is to be construed as necessarily reflecting the views of the Pacific Research Institute or as an attempt to thwart or aid the passage of any legislation.

©2017 Pacific Research Institute. All rights reserved. No part of this publication may be reproduced, stored in a retrieval system, or transmitted in any form or by any means, electronic, mechanical, photocopy, recording, or otherwise, without prior written consent of the publisher.

AN AMERICAN EDUCATION AGENDA

Top 15 Recommendations For Improving K-12 Education

LANCE IZUMI

TOP 15 RECOMMENDATIONS
FOR IMPROVING K-12 EDUCATION

TOP 5 FEDERAL RECOMMENDATIONS

1 SHRINK THE SIZE OF THE U.S. DEPARTMENT OF EDUCATION

2 APPOINT AN EFFECTIVENESS TASK FORCE TO REVIEW FEDERAL EDUCATION PROGRAMS

3 FEDERAL TAX CREDIT FOR SCHOOL CHOICE

4 REPEAL OBAMA-ERA POLICIES

5 WIDEN THE DISCUSSION OF SCHOOL CHOICE

TOP 10 STATE AND LOCAL RECOMMENDATIONS

1. **REPEAL AND REPLACE COMMON CORE**

2. **IMPROVE CHARTER SCHOOL LAWS**

3. **IMPLEMENT EXPANSIVE PRIVATE SCHOOL CHOICE PROGRAMS**

4. **VERGARA REFORMS: TEACHER TENURE, LAYOFF POLICIES, AND REMOVAL PROCEDURES**

5. **IMPROVE THE ENVIRONMENT FOR DIGITAL LEARNING TO SUCCEED**

6. **REFORM TEACHER EDUCATION AND PREPARATION PROGRAMS**

7. **INCREASE EDUCATION FINANCE TRANSPARENCY**

8. **CREATE STRONG ACCOUNTABILITY PLANS UNDER THE EVERY STUDENT SUCCEEDS ACT**

9. **IMPROVE SCHOOL SAFETY**

10. **EXPAND TEACHER CHOICE**

Introduction

The advent of a new administration in Washington presents a good opportunity to look afresh at the education landscape in America and see what areas are in need of the greatest reform and what those reforms may be and may entail. The following are a top-15 list of reforms that should be considered by education policymakers in Washington, state capitals and at the local level. Since education has historically been a state and local issue, more of the reform recommendations are directed at state and local policymakers.

FEDERAL RECOMMENDATION

Shrink the Size of the U.S. Department of Education

DISCUSSION

Since its creation, critics of the U.S. Department of Education have called for its elimination. Ronald Reagan famously campaigned on eliminating the department during the 1980 presidential race. In February 2017, Congressman Thomas Massie (R-KY) introduced a one-sentence bill to eliminate the department, which garnered national headlines, but which even Massie has admitted stands a slim chance of passage. However, while elimination may be a bridge too far, shrinking the size and scope of the department may be more attainable.

How could one shrink the size of the department? One way, which the Trump administration has proposed in its budget plan, is to eliminate certain programs.

For example, the proposed Trump budget called for the elimination of the $1.2 billion 21st Century Community Learning Centers program. The program establishes before- and after-school programs, plus summer programs, aimed at improving student academic outcomes. The Trump administration argued that "overall program performance data show that the program is not achieving its goal of helping students, particularly those who attend low-performing schools, meet challenging State academic standards."

"These data," concludes the administration, "strongly suggest that the 21st CCLC is not generating the benefits commensurate with an annual investment of more than $1 billion in limited Federal education funds."

All in all, the proposed Trump education budget would reduce the federal education discretionary budget by around $9 billion, from $68 billion to $59 billion. Besides cutting programs and spending, another way to shrink the department would be to change the structure of the department itself and offload various programs and responsibilities to other federal agencies. Various education analysts and writers on both the right and left have noted this option.

For example, in a discussion of Congressman Massie's bill, Eric Boehm at the libertarian Reason Foundation wrote that one response to the bill would be to shift programs from the Education Department to other agencies:

> "Some programs in the Department of Education could be shifted to other parts of the government. Student loan programs could run through the Treasury, or job training programs could be moved into the Department of Labor, in the same way that school lunch programs are already run by the Department of Agriculture, for example."[1]

Alexander Holt, writing for the centrist New America think tank, also says that the federal student loan and grant programs "could be moved to the Department of Treasury," which, he points out, is "something a number of experts have proposed."[2]

On the K-12 side, Holt notes, the massive Title I program for disadvantaged students and the IDEA program for students with disabilities could be turned "into HHS-administered block grants, and give the Department of Justice power to monitor patterns in school spending and take action against states if they suspect that federal funding is being diverted."

"The block grant approach," Holt points out, "would make it harder for the federal government to use Title I as a hammer to craft state policy, which would be a welcome development for Republicans [and states]."[3]

In addition, vocational education programs could be administered by the Department of Labor since, as Holt says, "That agency is theoretically more focused on the challenges of workforce development in the 21st Century, and could make for a better fit for those funds than the K-12-focused Department of Education."[4]

Alternatively, given that "much workforce development funding actually happens through the Pell Grant program, which would now be administered through the Treasury," the Education Department's vocational-education funding could be moved into the Pell Grant Program, which would "allow students to access the program for the summer months, something that would be particularly useful for adult learners looking to gain new skills."[5]

Even Bruce Meredith, a former general counsel to the NEA-affiliated Wisconsin Education Association, observed in an op-ed article he co-authored with UMass-Dartmouth professor Mark Paige that the Department of Education's "essential tasks can be shifted to Health and Human Services and the Justice Department."[6]

Thus, short of outright elimination of the Department of Education, it is certainly possible to shrink the size of the department.

RECOMMENDATION

The Trump administration and Congress should consider restructuring the U.S. Department of Education to reduce the number of programs for which it is responsible.

FEDERAL RECOMMENDATION

2. Appoint an Effectiveness Task Force to Review Federal Education Programs

DISCUSSION

In April 2017, President Trump signed an executive order that required Secretary of Education Betsy DeVos to, according to *The Washington Post*, "study whether and how the federal government has overstepped its legal authority in K-12 schools."[7]

At the signing event, President Trump said, "Previous administrations have wrongfully forced states and schools to comply with federal whims and dictate what our kids are taught." However, he pointed out, "we know that local communities do it best and know it best."[8]

The executive order gives Secretary DeVos 300 days to conduct a review of regulations related to K-12 schools that are inconsistent with federal law. An internal Department of Education task force has been created to oversee the review.

President Trump is right to focus attention on the decades-long buildup of federal overreach in education policy. There are other things he can do to reverse this disturbing trend.

In his education budget proposal, the president sought to eliminate certain federal education programs because of their record of ineffectiveness. While very admirable, the budget proposals are by nature piecemeal efforts that lack the unifying force of a larger policy call-to-arms.

To provide that larger unifying force and to focus public attention on the long and ongoing legacy of failed federal education spending, the President could appoint a blue-ribbon task force or commission of independent experts to examine waste and ineffectiveness in federal education spending.

President Trump has already made use of the independent commission idea when he created his Presidential Commission on Election Integrity. And past presidents have used the independent commission to investigate key policy issues.

One of the most well known of these past presidential commissions is the Private Sector Survey on Cost Control, commonly called the Grace Commission, created by President Ronald Reagan. The commission's task was to identify waste and inefficiency in the federal government.

In its 1984 report to Congress, the Grace Commission identified $424 billion in savings over a three-year period. While the commission's specific recommendations were valuable in and of themselves, President Reagan used the commission's report as a tool to educate the American people on the overexpansion of the federal government and why his administration's efforts to roll back federal spending were correct and justified.[9]

An education Grace Commission focused on federal education programs would not only identify waste and ineffectiveness in federal education spending, it would also focus public attention on the role that Washington plays in education policy and programming.

While it is true that various government agencies, such as the U.S. Government Accountability Office, think tanks and other organizations and researchers have looked at aspects of the federal education-spending problem, few have attempted a comprehensive in-depth analysis with big-picture recommendations that would resonate outside Beltway and insider circles. An education Grace Commission report would be different and could significantly impact the education debate and the way the public views federal education efforts.

RECOMMENDATION

President Trump should appoint an independent task force or commission to review and analyze the effectiveness of federal education programs.

AMERICAN EDUCATION AGENDA 7

FEDERAL RECOMMENDATION

Federal Tax Credit for School Choice

DISCUSSION

During the 2016 presidential campaign, Donald Trump said that he wanted to devote $20 billion to school choice. A federal tax credit for school choice is one of the most promising ways for the president to follow through on his campaign commitment. As of the writing of this paper, the Trump administration has yet to reveal their ultimate school choice plans. Experts, however, have offered tax-credit options for the administration to consider.

Larry Mone, president of the Manhattan Institute, laid out one such possibility:

> Here's how such a proposal could work: Individuals and corporations that chose to donate to eligible K-12 scholarship-granting organizations would be able to lower their tax bill by the amount of the donation. The size of the tax credit could be capped, and the scholarships funded by the donations could be targeted to low- and middle-income families [to pay for tuition at private schools].
>
> Legislation could also potentially limit the total combined amount of tax credits allowed in a calendar year. Florida's program, for example, hands out tax credits on a straightforward first-come, first-served basis.[10]

Currently, according to the American Federation of Children, "Publicly-supported tax credit scholarship programs are currently in place in 17 states and educate over 250,000 children, mostly from low-income families."[11]

Mone notes that while some have advised that any federal tax-credit program be limited to the 17 states that already have scholarship-granting programs, it is states like New York and New Jersey, which do not have such programs, "where tax credits could help the most."[12] The availability of tax credits, however, could act as an incentive for states to create tax-credit scholarship-granting programs.

Nat Malkus of the American Enterprise Institute argues that the tax credit should not be limited to just the 17 states that already have scholarship-granting programs, but proposes making allowance for new programs created by other states:

> The budget resolution could include federal tax credits for individual and corporate donations to non-profit scholarship-granting organizations (SGOs) operating within taxpayers' state of residence or operation. Residents could only qualify for the credit if their state runs or creates a school choice program that receives state credits or funding, and only state residents would receive scholarships.[13]

"These participation limits," says Markus, "would ensure states have skin in the game and vested interests in developing program specifics that make sense for their local contexts."[14]

According to Malkus, there are many pluses to such a plan:

> It would extend choice in multiple ways. It would bolster existing state programs and prevent undue federal interference. More states would develop school choice programs. They would also develop more different programs, with different degrees of success, which would let states learn from each other. It would also encourage states to cultivate the supply side of the school choice equation—the stock of private schools—which is frequently overlooked in these discussions. State influence on the supply side may seem limited, but creating clear rules for participation, sustainable programs, and constituencies to defend them when political winds change are essential to building the private investments, philanthropic interest, and entrepreneurial confidence that can make or break the supply of private schools.[15]

Like Larry Mone at the Manhattan Institute, other choice advocates want the tax credit to be available in all 50 states immediately. Thomas Carroll, head of the New York-based Invest in Education Coalition, makes the argument:

First, the tax credit should apply to all fifty states. The federal tax code is universal, and so should be a scholarship tax credit. Some on the Right would have the tax credit only operate in some states, not others. Any opt-in feature would limit the tax credit to red states and leave out millions of students who need choice in blue and purple states. This would be a huge mistake.[16]

Also, the American Federation of Children states, "A well-designed federal tax credit would help expand programs in current states and offer educational freedom in states without programs, including states where legislatures controlled by special interests refuse to pass tax credit scholarship laws."[17]

While there is disagreement within the choice movement over the initial breadth of a federal tax credit, there is greater agreement on other issues. The American Federation of Children notes that any tax credit should have certain components:

> It should not come with a host of regulations to burden private schools and suppress participation. It should include common sense financial and academic accountability to ensure appropriate use of taxpayer funds and to show participating students are making academic progress. It should be a parent-centered program in which recipients have the freedom to take their scholarship to any participating private school. It should also have an income eligibility threshold that is high enough to help struggling working- and middle-class families participate.[18]

In the end, the overarching issue is that a federal tax credit for school choice is the best way for Washington to offer parents and their children greater opportunities in education. As John Kirtley, vice chair of the American Federation of Children, notes, "Real windows of opportunity to advance bold public policy that truly puts the interest of students first are rare."[19] With the federal tax credit, however, that window is now.

RECOMMENDATION

Enact a federal tax credit for individuals and corporations making charitable contributions to non-profit scholarship-granting organizations.

FEDERAL RECOMMENDATION

Repeal Obama-Era Policies

DISCUSSION

The Obama administration made sweeping changes to education policy through the use of Education Department directives, regulations, and other other policy tools. Take, for instance, its efforts to reduce the use of suspension as a response to student violence and misbehavior.

Citing statistics showing that a disparately large number of suspensions were meted out to minority students, the Obama administration's Office of Civil Rights (OCR) at the U.S. Department of Education and the Civil Rights Division of the U.S. Department of Justice issued a so-called "Dear Colleague" letter in 2014 that warned school districts:

> Schools also violate Federal law when they evenhandedly implement facially neutral polices and practices that, although not adopted with the intent to discriminate, nonetheless have an unjustified effect of discriminating against students on the basis of race. The resulting discriminatory effect is commonly referred to as "disparate impact."[20]

Discipline policies that can raise disparate impact concerns, according to the government enforcers, could include "mandatory suspension, expulsion, or citation."[21]

In the wake of the Obama administration's warning, the OCR opened civil rights investigations into a number of school districts, including the Oakland Unified School District and the Oklahoma City Public Schools. Both districts agreed to reduce greatly their use of suspensions.[22] There are major problems, however, with the federal anti-suspension crusade.

First of all, using disparate impact as a gauge for racial discrimination turns out to be empirically wrong. A landmark 2014 study by criminology and economics professors from the University of Cincinnati, Florida State University and the University of Texas at Dallas, which was published in the *Journal of Criminal Justice*, examined the problem behavior of suspended students prior to their suspensions.

Using long-term data from the Early Childhood Longitudinal Study, which covered a massive 21,000 children, the researchers examined "whether measures of prior problem behavior could account for the differences in suspension between both whites and blacks." Their findings were eye-opening:

> The results of these analyses were straightforward: The inclusion of a measure of prior problem behavior reduced to statistical insignificance the odds differentials in suspensions between black and white youth.
>
> Thus, our results indicate that odds differentials in suspensions are likely produced by pre-existing behavioral problems of youth that are imported into the classroom, that cause classroom disruptions, and that trigger disciplinary measures by teachers and school officials. Differences in rates of suspension between racial groups thus appear to be a function of differences in problem behaviors that emerge early in life, that remain relatively stable over time, and that materialize in the classroom.[23]

Thus, the racial disparity in suspension rates between African-American and white students can be explained by the prior problem behavior of the students, and is not the result of racism and cultural biases harbored by teachers and school officials. "Our results suggest," the researchers conclude, "that the association between school suspensions and blacks and whites reflects long-standing behavioral differences between youth and that, at least in the aggregate, the use of suspensions may not be as racially biased as many have argued."[24]

The study's authors admonished "numerous authors, interest groups, and government agencies including the Department of Justice," which "have used the racial differential in suspension rates as *prima facie* evidence of teacher or school district bias against black youth."

They observed that "great liberties have been taken in linking racial differences in suspensions to racial discrimination."[25] The researchers caution "against the clear motivations of some scholars and activists to frame race differences in school suspensions as only a matter of discrimination or cultural bias, and especially when framed as a civil rights issue with all the corresponding threats of litigation by the federal government."[26]

Further, and most important for parents, there is evidence that disruptive students left in the classroom have a negative impact on the learning of their fellow students. According to a study by researchers at the University of California at Davis and the University of Pittsburgh, leaving disruptive students in a classroom has "a statistically significant negative effect on their peers' reading and math test scores."[27]

In addition, a single disruptive student "also significantly increases misbehavior of other students in the classroom," causing them to commit 16 percent more infractions than they otherwise would.[28]

The researchers conclude that their findings "provide strong evidence of the validity of the 'bad apple' peer effects model, which hypothesizes that a single disruptive student can negatively affect the outcomes for all other students in the classroom."[29]

Thus, the Obama-era anti-suspension directive ties the hands of local schools as they try to deal with disruptive students. While some anti-suspension activists have advocated non-suspension strategies such as restorative justice methods, which involve talking through problems with disruptive students, there is little proof of their success. Thus, suspension should be available as a strategy to punish student misbehavior, to keep order in the classroom, and to ensure learning for all students.

Another Obama-era change that concerns many parents and grassroots education activists is the late 2011 regulations published by the Education Department relating to the Family Educational Rights and Privacy Act (FERPA), which is a federal law that gives parents certain protections regarding their children's education records.

In email correspondences with the author of this paper, Ze'ev Wurman, a senior policy advisor in the Education Department during the George W. Bush administration, said that the Obama-era regulations re-defined who is an "authorized representative" that can receive private student data and what is an "education program" that is a proper justification for receiving such data.

Wurman explained: "Specifically, 'education program' did not need anymore to be administered by educational agencies or institutions or be narrowly tailored for education, but, rather, anything broadly and even tangentially touching on education would qualify. So, Department of Labor, Health and Human Services, or any private company, could, in principle, qualify."

Further, Wurman noted that that federal contracts signed with the testing groups putting together the new Common Core-aligned tests "explicitly specified that they must provide student-level data to the Education Department— never before did the Education Department get individual student-level data." Previously, "it was explicitly prohibited to get such data even if the state offered."

As a bit of history, Wurman pointed out that when Barack Obama became president, he and his secretary of education, Arne Duncan, "had a lot of connections with the high tech community and it wanted access to [student-level] data to: (a) make tools that can track and 'predict' student achievement, so they can sell them to school districts hot after monitoring every student under No Child Left Behind; (b) sell technology-based curricular solutions to schools and districts." "So," explained Wurman, "they needed access to such data to build and tune their tools." For these reasons, Duncan almost immediately pushed for new regulations to FERPA, and he ended up sacking the head of the office overseeing FERPA who "refused to lower privacy protections (as the law really insisted)."

Wurman observed that many interests in and out of government want access to student data for their own self-interested purposes. Thus, there would be significant resistance to changing the Obama-era FERPA regulations. "Yet," he concluded, "it should be done, reverting to the [prior] late 2008 [FERPA] language."

There have been efforts in Washington to change the Obama-era FERPA regulations. U.S. Representative Todd Rokita (R-IN) introduced HR 3157, the Student Privacy Protection Act, which addressed the student privacy problems in the regulations. Rokita's bill has yet to pass.

While Barack Obama was president, Wurman said that it was deemed "smarter to try a congressional path" than try to change the regulations in-house at the Education Department. Now, however, with Donald Trump as president, the situation has changed dramatically.

Thus, Wurman advised Education Secretary Betsy DeVos to rescind the Obama-era FERPA regulations and to make the argument "that she is simply undoing Obama's opening the flood gates for student personal information flowing to private and non-educational players," which "should make a serious impact on the grassroots, that is incensed by it."

RECOMMENDATION

The Trump administration should rescind Obama-era policies such as those relating to student suspension and student privacy.

FEDERAL RECOMMENDATION

Widen the Discussion of School Choice

DISCUSSION

When Congress passed and President Obama signed the Every Student Succeeds Act in 2015, some of the power of the federal government in education was pulled back and greater control and autonomy was given to the states. This development impacts Secretary Betsy DeVos' ability to act on issues such as her core support for school choice.

Elizabeth Mann, a fellow in governance studies at the Brown Center on Education Policy at the Brookings Institution, points out that given the limitations put on the U.S. Department of Education and the secretary of education by ESSA, it will not be easy to implement her school choice agenda:

> In short, even though DeVos is an outspoken advocate of school choice, the Secretary of Education lacks the authority to simply mandate policy changes to states. As a result, if she is to implement her policy agenda, it will require cooperation from governors, chief state school officers, and state school boards.[30]

Further, says Mann, "Without the 'carrot' of funding under Race to the Top [federal grant program] or the 'stick' of NCLB mandates [on accountability], DeVos lacks leverage over governors who are not inclined to implement an aggressive school choice agenda."[31]

While Secretary DeVos does not have the power on paper of previous secretaries, she still retains the power of the bully pulpit and the ability to shift and focus discussion and debate. Indeed, Secretary DeVos has said that given that "the federal role in funding education is certainly negligible as compared to the states," then, "I think there is an opportunity for the federal government to set a tone and I'm working to continue to do so every opportunity I have to talk about this."[32]

One place that Secretary DeVos could set the tone is in her favorite policy area of school choice. She could use the bully pulpit afforded her as secretary to widen the terms of discussion of school choice.

For years, school choice advocates have relied on arguments that involve showing how students in school choice programs fare better academically than comparable students in regular public schools. While very important, this mono-dimensional argument ignores the many other non-academic, non-performance reasons why parents may want choice options for their children.

As detailed in Pacific Research Institute's 2017 book *The Corrupt Classroom: Bias, Indoctrination, Violence, and Social Engineering Show Why America Needs School Choice*, America's public schools are becoming increasingly politicized, less safe, socially biased, and mismanaged. The evidence of this transformation stretches from coast to coast:

- In 2016, teachers in California and North Carolina compared Donald Trump to Adolf Hitler, a Texas teacher pretended to assassinate President Trump in a video, and a New Hampshire teacher dressed up as Donald Trump and danced to a profane anti-Trump rap song.

- California's history and social studies curriculum frameworks conspicuously fail to mention monumental communist atrocities, such as the 20 million people killed by the Soviet Union and the 65 million killed by Maoist China.

- According to the latest federal statistics, 65 percent of public schools reported one or more incidents of violence – translating to 757,000 crimes.

- In 2014, teachers and school staff reportedly committed 781 sex crimes.

- Facing bankruptcy, the Los Angeles school board still gave expensive health benefits to part-time workers, and now faces a massive $1.4 billion deficit.

- Pennsylvania parents have sued their school district because the district's transgender policies force children to change in a locker room with biological members of the opposite sex.

- Parents in different states have complained and filed lawsuits regarding the unfairness and lack of balance in teaching religion in the classroom.

If public schools insist on educating students under such conditions, parents and their children should have the right and the tools to exit the public-school system for educational alternatives that better meet their needs and preferences. And Secretary DeVos can use her bully pulpit to highlight these reasons, which strike home with parents.

In addition, by focusing on these non-academic reasons for school choice, the secretary can also highlight areas where public schools need to do better.

President Trump has been hugely effective in pushing his policy agenda in areas such as public safety and illegal immigration by focusing on the individual victims of crimes and illegal activities. So, too, Secretary DeVos could highlight the real parent and student victims of politicized classrooms, unsafe schools, and socially engineered curricula and policies.

A shocking YouGov poll found that only 25 percent of millennials believe that living in a democracy is essential, down from 75 percent in their grandparents' generation.[33] Marion Smith, executive director of the Victims of Communism Memorial Foundation, recently wrote that young people have been influenced by educational systems to oppose free-market economics, to whitewash the human toll of Marxism, and to turn to socialism and other forms of extremist ideologies.[34]

Thus, beyond test scores, it is the obvious corruption in America's classrooms that is the most convincing argument for freedom of choice in education.

RECOMMENDATIONS

Secretary DeVos and her team should use the bully pulpit of their positions to discuss the many non-academic reasons why parents would want school choice options.

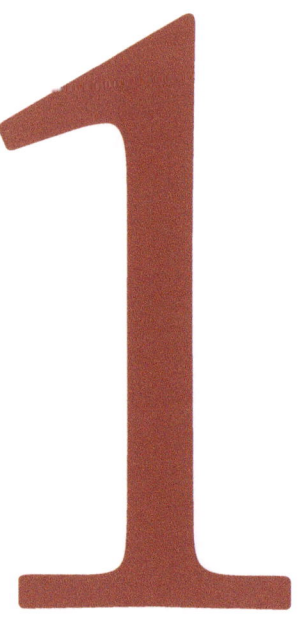

STATE AND LOCAL RECOMMENDATION

Repeal and Replace Common Core

DISCUSSION

Common Core is a national education standards, testing and curriculum regime that most states have adopted in one form or another. Created by a small group of education insiders in 2009-10 under the imprimatur of the Council of Chief State School Officers and the National Governors Association, and pushed on the states by the Obama administration's use of federal dollars as incentives to adopt, Common Core has failed to deliver in academic achievement.

On the 2015 National Assessment for Educational Progress, often referred to as the nation's report card, student scores in English and math declined significantly. According to Peggy Carr, acting commissioner of the National Center for Education Statistics, "In mathematics, for the first time since the early 1990s, there were declines nationally in scores at both grades 4 and 8 since the last assessment." Further, "Average mathematics scores were lower for students across the performance range, from high performers to lower performers."[35]

Specifically, noted Carr:

> At the state level, mathematics results were mixed—at grade 4, average scores were higher in 2015 than in 2013 in 3 states and/or jurisdictions. In 30 states, however, the average score in mathematics was lower in at least one of the grades.
>
> At grade 8, national average scores were lower than in 2013 in both mathematics and reading and this was generally true for students across the performance range. The average grade 8 reading score was higher in 1 state; the average mathematics score did not increase in any state. Scores were lower in 26 states in either mathematics or reading, or in both subjects.[36]

Carr commented, "This isn't a pattern we saw coming. It was an unexpected downturn."[37] Others, however, were not surprised that the NAEP scores declined.

Jamie Gass, director of the Center for School Reform at the Boston-based Pioneer Institute, which has been a key intellectual critic of Common Core, observed, "Five years into the overhyped and academically mediocre Common Core, the 2015 NAEP data makes clear that the initiative has failed students miserably."[38]

Looking at the NAEP results in Massachusetts, which has historically been a test-score leader, Gass pointed out:

> Even the nation's highest performer, Massachusetts, has dropped out of its number one position on the eighth grade 2015 NAEP reading rankings, and overall the impact on the state has been to drive *down* student achievement. Together with the national data, this is a pretty damning indication of the real-life effect of Common Core's cutting higher quality classic literature, poetry, and drama. It's just another example of a Beltway-driven K-12 education reform failure.[39]

Historically low-performing states, such as California, also saw further declines. The average score of California eighth graders declined in both reading and math from 2013 to 2015. Especially concerning are the results for minority students.

On the 2015 NAEP eighth-grade reading exam, 72 percent of California eighth-graders failed to achieve proficiency. Worse, 84 percent of African-American and 82 percent of Latino eighth graders failed to hit proficiency.

The results were worse on the math exam, where 73 percent of California eighth graders overall, 86 percent of African Americans and 87 percent of Latinos failed to achieve proficiency.

Yet, it is important to point out that the scores of white students also declined. As *Education Week* noted: "White students' scores declined in both 8th grade subjects as well. Black and Hispanic students' scores were down in both math and reading for 8th grade."[40]

"The only plausible explanation for such an unprecedented broad national decline [in NAEP scores]," observed Ze'ev Wurman, former senior education policy advisor under President George W. Bush and top standards expert, "is the Common Core." Further, "for the first time in 10 years we see drops in 12th-grade student achievement in both math and reading."[41]

Wurman highlighted Common Core's failure to prepare students for college:

> We should remember that Common Core was imposed on the nation under the excuse of expecting college readiness from all students. The fraction of college-ready 12th graders dropped since 2013, from 39% to 37% in math and from 38% to 37% in reading. Even more interestingly, NAEP scores show that less than 50% of students taking pre-calculus class by 12th grade are deemed college ready. Only when students take a calculus class by grade 12, more than 50% of them reach college readiness by high school graduation. Perhaps this is a good time to remind everyone that Common Core – in its fullness – does not prepare students even for a full pre-calculus class."[42]

The poor performance of America's children under Common Core are the natural byproduct of the controversial teaching methods promoted by Common Core-aligned curricula that emphasize convoluted math strategies, group learning, and how students get an answer rather than whether they get the right answer.

In the wake of the enactment of the federal Every Students Succeeds Act (ESSA), congressional leaders have boasted that Washington no longer requires states to keep Common Core. But that does not mean that Common Core simply goes away. Individual states adopted Common Core and it is therefore each state's responsibility to address the failings of Common Core.

Writing in *The Daily Caller*, reporter Blake Neef correctly noted, "What ESSA does do is prohibit the federal government from using various tactics that encouraged, but did not require, the adoption of Common Core at the state level."[43]

"By extension," wrote Neef, "it wasn't federal requirements that were keeping Common Core held in place around the country, but rather, "it was support from both Democrats and Republicans, who have defeated several repeal efforts around the country."[44]

The bottom line, according to Neef: "repeal must be done state by state across the country."[45]

The good news is that if states repeal Common Core there were several excellent pre-Common Core state standards that could be used as replacements. Massachusetts, for example, was a leader in the quality of its pre-Common Core standards.[46]

RECOMMENDATIONS

- For states that have adopted them, state policymakers should repeal the Common Core standards.

- States should not simply re-brand the Common Core standards, as some states have done, and claim that they are legitimate replacements for Common Core.

- States should look at rigorous high-quality pre-Common Core state standards, such as those in Massachusetts, as models for their post-Common Core standards.

STATE AND LOCAL RECOMMENDATION

Improve Charter School Laws

DISCUSSION

Charter schools are publicly funded schools that are independent of the local school district in which they are located. They are free of many of the regulations that often tie up regular public schools, but, in return, are more accountable for the outcomes of their students. They are often run by parents, teachers, and organizations ranging from universities to non-public management entities.

Charter schools have been the subject of much research. For example, in 2015, the National Charter School Resource Center, funded by the U.S. Department of Education, analyzed the best empirical research on charter schools and found "that charter school students perform as well or better in math and reading as compared with the comparison group."[47] The comparison group was composed of students who lost a lottery to attend a charter school and then usually attended a regular public school.

Further, a groundbreaking 2017 Temple University study of 900,000 students found that charter schools that co-located on the premises of an existing regular public school ended up improving the performance of the regular public school students. Also, the regular public school's safety, climate, and morale improve.[48]

In the early 1990s, Minnesota and California were the first states to adopt laws allowing for the creation of charter schools. Now only a dwindling few states have failed to enact charter school laws. Not all charter laws, however, are created equal.

The National Alliance for Public Charter Schools (NAPCS) puts out a ranking of state charter laws. These rankings are based on 20-factor criteria, ranging from no caps on the growth of charter schools in the state to the availability of multiple authorizers for charter schools to requiring performance-based charter contracts to clear processes for renewal, nonrenewal, and revocation decisions.[49]

There are many states that have weak charter laws on their books that could be improved significantly.

For example, Maryland was ranked last on NAPCS' list. According to NAPCS, although Maryland does not cap charter school growth, "it allows only local school district authorizers and provides little autonomy, insufficient accountability, and inequitable funding to charters."[50] Further, Maryland does not have clear processes for renewal, nonrenewal, and revocation decisions.[51]

In contrast, number one-ranked Indiana "includes multiple authorizers (and) provides a fair amount of autonomy and accountability." Further, Indiana has made strides to provide more equitable funding for charters.[52]

The bottom line is that states can craft their charter school laws to give wide choice to parents, ensure high quality education for students, and give incentive for the regular public school system to improve.

RECOMMENDATIONS

- States that have not yet enacted laws allowing charter schools should do so.
- States that have charter-school laws on the books should review their laws and improve them by looking at model charter-school laws issued by the National Alliance of Public Charter Schools and others.

STATE AND LOCAL RECOMMENDATION

3 Implement Expansive Private School Choice Programs

DISCUSSION

There are many reasons for state leaders to implement expansive private school choice programs such as education savings accounts, vouchers, and tax credits.

For many years, school choice advocates have pointed to the prepondeance of positive results from high-quality empirical studies showing that students benefit academically from private school choice programs.

Greg Forster, in his 2016 study "A Win-Win Solution: The Empirical Evidence for School Choice," written for EdChoice (formerly the Friedman Foundation for Educational Choice), found:

> Eighteen empirical studies have examined academic outcomes for school choice participants using random assignment, the gold standard of social science. Of those, 14 find choice improves student outcomes: six find all students benefit and eight find some benefit and some are not visibly affected. Two studies find no visible effect, and two studies find Louisiana's voucher program—where most of the eligible private schools were scared away from the program by an expectation of hostile future action from regulators—had a negative effect. [53]

Patrick Wolf and colleagues at the University of Arkansas analyzed the best research on voucher programs worldwide and found "that voucher programs globally tend to positively impact test scores."[54]

Yet, while empirical data on academic performance under school choice programs is important, it is not the only reason that states should enact expansive school choice programs. As detailed in Pacific Research Institute's 2017 book *The Corrupt Classroom: Bias, Indoctrination, Violence, and Social Engineering Show Why America Needs School Choice*, there are many non-student-performance reasons why parents want private school choice options.[55]

For example, parents are, for obvious reasons, concerned about the safety of their children when they go to school. If they feel that their children may be harmed because of gangs, bullying, rogue teachers, unhealthy peer culture, or lax school discipline policies, parents will want to find safer schooling options, regardless of their performance on standardized tests.

Also, many parents are rightly concerned about the growing politicization of the classroom. Outbursts from educators during the recent presidential election are but the tip of the political-bias iceberg. Far from being mere anecdotal incidents—and there are a lot of those—political bias is becoming systemic in public school systems and has turned many public schools into indoctrination centers for progressive ideologies and causes.

Curricula are often chosen by school officials with little input from parents, who only find out about offensive materials when their children bring home their textbooks.

Further, if parents find that school officials ignore their concerns, then it becomes sensible for them to seek out schooling alternatives.

And if education officials mismanage resources causing negative impacts on students, then why should parents want to continue to send their children to schools run by those officials?

All of these reasons, plus many others, have nothing to do with the academic performance of schools and students, yet are understandable reasons for parents to demand that they be empowered to choose different schooling options for their children.

In recent years, some states have enacted expansive private school choice programs. Nevada and Arizona, for example, have enacted near-universal education savings accounts programs, where government funds are placed in individual accounts that parents can access to pay for specified education expenses, including private school tuition. Other states, however, have state laws that impede or prevent the creation of private school choice programs.

Thus, while Wisconsin is the home of pioneering Milwaukee private school choice voucher program, next door in Michigan there is no private school choice because as U.S. Secretary of Education Betsy DeVos, a native Michigander, notes, "Michigan is limited in its offering of choice to having only charter schools so there's no private school choice in Michigan largely due to the fact that we have a very restrictive Blaine Amendment in Michigan."

Blaine Amendments are provisions in state constitutions that prevent state funds from going to any religiously affiliated organization or institution. For example, Missouri's Blaine Amendment prohibits public funding of any "school, academy, seminary, college, university, or other institution of learning controlled by any religious creed, church or sectarian denomination."

California's Blaine Amendment is similar to the Missouri provision: "No public money shall ever be appropriated for the support of any sectarian or denominational school, or any school not under the exclusive control of the officers of the public schools."

Around three-dozen states have Blaine Amendments. Some state courts have used state Blaine amendments to invalidate school choice programs.

In 2015, the Colorado Supreme Court used the state's Blaine Amendment to stop a voucher program enacted by Douglas County. However, the Nevada Supreme Court decided that Nevada's Blaine Amendment did not invalidate that state's education savings account program.

The recent U.S. Supreme Court decision in *Trinity Lutheran of Columbia v. Pauley* held open the possibility that the court might eventually strike down the Blaine Amendments as violations of the U.S. Constitution. Until that time, states still have the power to repeal their state Blaine Amendments and other laws that prevent the enactment of private school choice programs.

While repealing state constitutional provisions such as Blaine Amendments will not be easy, the large public support for expansive private school choice programs should push state lawmakers to do so. According to a 2017 nationwide poll conducted for the publication *Education Next,* a significant plurality, 45 percent to 37 percent, of those polled favored a universal voucher, which would grant parents government funding to pay for private school tuition for their children.[56]

The support for private school choice is, surprisingly, even greater in places like deep blue California. A 2017 poll by the respected Public Policy Institute of California found that a large majority of Californians support school choice vouchers.[57]

In the PPIC poll, 60 percent of adults said they favored tax-funded vouchers, while two-thirds of public school parents, 66 percent, supported vouchers.[58]

The support was even higher among African Americans and Latinos – 73 percent and 69 percent, respectively.[59]

Thus, there is strong support for expansive private school choice tools. It is up to state lawmakers to respond.

RECOMMENDATIONS

- Enact expansive school choice programs such as Arizona's education savings accounts.

- Repeal restrictive laws, such as state Blaine Amendments, that impede enactment of expansive school choice programs.

STATE AND LOCAL RECOMMENDATION

Vergara Reforms: Teacher Tenure, Layoff Policies, and Removal Procedures

DISCUSSION

Many states have laws that make it easy and quick for teachers to obtain tenure, promote last-in-first-out layoff policies, and make it difficult and expensive to fire bad teachers. These issues were at the heart of the much-watched *Vergara v. California* case.

The case, which was initiated in California's state courts, featured nine student plaintiffs, represented by Students Matter, a non-profit education organization. The students argued that California's short probationary time—18 months—before teachers received tenure allowed too many ineffective teachers to remain on the job permanently.

In court testimony, Harvard University Professor Raj Chetty, one of the nation's top experts on identifying bad teachers, said that, based on his research, "being assigned to a highly ineffective teacher generates significant harm in the long term" and being subjected to multiple ineffective teachers in a row "would substantially reduce your chances of attending college" and "substantially reduce students' earnings."[60]

Chetty criticized the 18-month probation in the tenure statute saying it "is inadequate time to fully assess a teacher's effectiveness and hence that short probationary period has a negative, detrimental effect on student learning."[61]

Former Sacramento City Unified School District Superintendent Jonathan Raymond described the dance-of-the-lemons practices he had to employ to cope with the tenure law. He tried to minimize the "damage that grossly ineffective teachers have on students" by moving bad teachers up to three dozen times to different schools so as "to minimize the amount of time and the amount of children they [had] on a regular basis."[62] The Sacramento district spent nearly $1 million to move bad teachers into the substitute teacher pool to keep them out of the classroom as much as possible.

Also, the students argued that teacher layoff policies, where teachers with the least seniority were laid off first regardless of whether they were more effective than more senior teachers, hurt students whose learning is dependent on quality teachers.

Discussing the last-in-first-out statute, Bhavini Bhakta, a former teacher of the year in Southern California, testified that she lost four teaching jobs in eight years because of the law. In emotional testimony, she said, "I just felt like no matter what work I did in the classroom or how hard I worked that none of it mattered because a seniority date mattered way more than how much I did for kids, or what principals would say about me, or what parents would say about me." With frustration, she said, "Like, none of it mattered. Nothing … And, all that mattered was my hire date."[63]

Finally, the students said that teacher dismissal processes that cost school districts up to half a million dollars to dismiss a single bad teacher resulted in ineffective or even dangerous teachers remaining in classrooms.

Bill Kappenhagen, former principal at Burton High School in San Francisco, testified that because the dismissal process is so burdensome he had to take the drastic action of closing down the music program at the school in order to remove an extremely ineffective teacher from the classroom.[64]

Then-Los Angeles Superintendent John Deasy testified that the dismissal statutes require "volumes of documentation" in a process that can take years and which usually costs between $250,000 to $450,000 per attempted dismissal.[65]

In 2014, California Superior Court Judge Rolf Treu ruled that the state's teacher tenure, layoff and dismissal laws violated the state's constitutional guarantee of a quality education for every student. Judge Treu based his decision on compelling trial testimony, much of it from students, which he said, "shocks the conscience."[66]

At the time, it was reported that many states, such as Minnesota, New Jersey and Connecticut, were watching to see how the *Vergara* case would influence their laws.

However, a state appellate court reversed Judge Treu's ruling and the California Supreme Court failed to hear an appeal from the student plaintiffs. Yet, those setbacks do not prevent states from addressing the issues in *Vergara* through legislation.

In the wake of *Vergara*, Republican legislators in California offered up a package of bills that would have extended the number of probationary years for beginning teachers before they could receive tenure, eliminated last-in-first-out layoff policies, and revamped teacher evaluations to make them more frequent, more informative, and based on more objective criteria.

All states that have *Vergara*-type laws or polices should implement such reforms. As Raylene Monterroza, one of the student plaintiffs, has said, "We deserve better, all of us, in every school, in every grade, in every ZIP code."[67]

RECOMMENDATIONS

- States with short probationary periods should lengthen them so they have a better idea about whether beginning teachers will become high-quality teachers.

- State teacher layoff policies should be based on teacher-quality factors rather than mere seniority.

- Streamline dismissal procedures for ineffective teachers.

STATE AND LOCAL RECOMMENDATION

Improve the Environment for Digital Learning to Succeed

DISCUSSION

The technology revolution that continues to sweep through society also impacts the classroom. Improved computer hardware and innovative software make digital education an increasingly viable and potentially successful way for students to learn. However, it is still an emerging field that faces significant challenges.

One of the most promising types of digital education is blended learning. Michael Horn of the Christensen Institute observes: "K-12 blended learning is at its simplest, the mix of online learning and brick-and-mortar schools with teachers." The term "online learning" is learning from sources on the Internet, including books, videos, lessons and software.

More specifically, Horn says blended learning "is a formal education program in which a student learns in part online with some element of control over the time, place, path, and/or pace, in part in a supervised brick-and-mortar location away from home, and what a student does online is connected to what they do offline."[68]

There are numerous examples of individual schools that have used blended learning models to raise student achievement.

Grimmway Academy, an elementary public charter school in rural Arvin, California uses a blended-learning rotation model where students spend part of the day in traditional classrooms and then rotate to a computer lab where they use software programs such as Compass Learning for math and English, Reading Express and myON Reading to receive personalized instruction tailored to the individual interests and needs of the student. Based on the data generated by the software programs, teachers can pinpoint students' learning problems and assist those students in overcoming their learning obstacles.

The performance of Grimmway's mostly low-income Hispanic students under California's former STAR testing system was impressive. More than eight out of ten students in a number of grade levels scored at or above the proficient level in mathematics.

Summit Public Schools in Sunnyvale in California's Silicon Valley uses a blended-learning "flex" model. Cognitive skills such as writing are taught by teachers, but students also spend 16 hours a week acquiring other skills and knowledge through the use of the school's online resources.

Key to student learning are so-called topic playlists, which include guided practice problems, presentation, videos and more. Students take short assessments to determine if they have mastered the content and can then move on to new topics.

According to *U.S. News and World Report,* which did a lengthy story on Summit in 2017, each student has "a Google Chromebook and a dashboard that shows where they are on each subject: topics they have mastered turn green, those they still need to master are red." "They work on what they choose," said the article, "at their own pace, using the playlist options that fit their learning style best." But, "their mentor teacher can always see where they are and nudge them if they're falling too far behind."

These technology-assisted innovations have resulted in Summit students considerably outperforming average California student proficiency levels.

A major Achilles heel for blended learning and other technology-assisted learning models has been lack of adequate teacher training.

High school teacher Catlin Tucker, author of the book *Blended Learning in Grades 4-12,* estimates that only 10 percent of teachers have some understanding of digital tools and how to use them.[69]

In Los Angeles, the expensive experiment to give students iPads for their schoolwork crashed and burned. While there were several reasons for the disaster, the U.S. Department of Education highlighted the fact that teachers were badly trained on how to use the iPad and the associated curriculum. According to a Los Angeles school district contractor: "Teachers were not trained in the system to manage the devices."

In contrast, in Singapore, all teacher trainees are required to take teacher-training coursework that will give them the skills to use technology to facilitate student learning. Thus, all secondary schools in Singapore use blended learning models, and, not coincidentally, Singapore is a world leader in classroom achievement.

Besides deficient teacher preparation, state policies have often not kept up with the advances in education technology.

For example, the National Governors Association (NGA) warns against "enrollment count," which refers to the number of students in a classroom for the entire school day on a particular date, as the basis for funding schools. Enrollment-based funding does not take into account students "participating in learning experiences outside the classroom such as work-force certificate programs, virtual courses, and blended courses."[70]

The goal should be student mastery over subject matter rather than mere seat time. The NGA says, "States may not be able to realize the full potential of education reform until the system's focus shifts from time-based inputs to student learning outputs tied to the mastery of content and skills." The NGA recommends that states, "Build flexibility into state policy to allow students to earn credit based on demonstrating mastery in classroom and in expanded learning opportunities."[71]

Along these lines, the respected International Association for Online Learning (iNACOL) issued a nine-point policy roadmap for states:

- Create innovation zones, which provide pioneering school districts with flexibility from state policies and requirements, in order to implement personalized learning models.

- Convene a competency-based education task force to identify barriers and opportunities, and to provide a feedback loop.

- Provide flexibility to school districts to allow students to earn credits on demonstrated mastery.

- Launch pilot programs and planning grants to support personalized, competency-based learning models.

- Create policies that enable multiple pathways to earning credits and to graduation.

- Ensure mastery by implementing proficiency-based diplomas.

- Redesign systems of assessments to support student-centered learning.

- Create next generation accountability models focused on enabling continuous improvement.

- Build local capacity to transform education, connecting districts with research and experts, technical assistance, specialized training and peer learning networks.[72]

Where types of digital education have had performance problems, then state policies can also be changed to address these issues.

Take virtual charter schools, for example. These are charter schools that offer instruction through the Internet and where the teacher and student are separate rather than together in a brick-and-mortar classroom. Thus, students may access their instruction while at home.

Recent research has shown that virtual charter schools have had significant student achievement problems. A study of Ohio virtual charter schools by the Fordham Institute found that virtual charter students perform worse than students who attend brick-and-mortar regular district public schools.[73]

The Fordham study recommends that states address such problems with a three-pronged approach:

- First, policy makers should adopt performance-based funding for e-schools. When students complete courses successfully and demonstrate that they have mastered the expected competencies, e-schools would get paid.

- Second, policy makers should explore ways to improve the fit between students and e-schools. . . .There is also a need for rigorous research that investigates which strategies are most effective at sustaining student engagement and lifting achievement in an online environment, especially for students who opt for virtual schools because they are frustrated with (or failing out of) other forms of schooling.

- Third, policy makers should support online course choice (also called "course access"), so that students interested in web-based learning aren't limited to full-time options.[74]

Michael Horn of the Christensen Institute, who largely agrees with Fordham's recommendations, says, however, that when it comes to funding virtual schools:

> A sounder way forward would give virtual schools some up-front funds for fixed administrative and technology costs (such as furnishing students with a laptop and home Internet connection), and then fund schools with a weighted per-pupil rate as students mastered competencies and made academic progress, which embeds performance funding in the formula and is similar to how New Hampshire's Virtual Learning Academy is funded. In other words, a student's academic progress would replace seat time—such as average daily attendance—as the measurement that determines funding levels. As a simple example, when a student mastered 10 percent of a course, the school would receive 10 percent of funding for that course; when the student mastered the next 10 percent, the school would receive the next 10 percent of funds. External state assessments could be used to make sure schools' more micro-assessments of learning were rigorous and valid.[75]

Horn's policymaking bottom line on virtual schools: "Harnessing their benefits while reining in their downsides is critical."[76]

RECOMMENDATIONS

- States should push public university schools of education to offer and require training in how to use and teach with digital tools.

- States should review their digital education policies and regulations, and follow the recommendations for reform put forward by iNACOL, the Fordham Institute, and the Christensen Institute (see discussion above).

STATE AND LOCAL RECOMMENDATION

Reform Teacher Education and Preparation Programs

DISCUSSION

Much research shows that ineffective teachers have a significantly negative impact on the learning and academic achievement of children. Yet, many people, from lawmakers to parents to the public, fail to then ask what produced those bad teachers in the first place. The answer, however, is quite clear: in many cases, teacher education and training programs bear much responsibility.

The Education Consumers Federation, headed by East Tennessee State University professor of education psychology John E. Stone, observes:

> The larger problem, however, is that the pre-service training given teachers is often inadequate and in some cases detrimental. Teaching practices founded on theory and craft knowledge, not experimental evidence, are typical fare. Worse, proven practices that are contrary to favored theory may be denigrated as boring or emotionally damaging.

> In-service professional development can be equally problematic. Teaching innovations that are as little tested as the practices they replace are commonly touted as breakthroughs in pedagogy. The educational fads that have become an unfortunate hallmark of public schooling often originate in schools of education.

> Teacher preparation programs are most often housed in colleges of education and, like other professional training programs, they are accountable for meeting the broad standards set by accrediting bodies and professional societies. With the exception of a few states, however, they are not accountable for the effectiveness of the practices taught to their graduates.[77]

In addition, the National Council for Teacher Quality (NCTQ) found widespread lack of rigor among university teacher preparation programs:

> Using evidence from more than 500 higher education institutions that turn out nearly half of the nation's new teachers each year, we find that in a majority of institutions (58 percent), grading standards for teacher candidates are much lower than for students in other majors on the same campus.
>
> Second, we find a strong link between high grades and a lack of rigorous coursework, with the primary cause being assignments that fail to develop the critical skills and knowledge every new teacher needs.
>
> . . .
>
> These results are a wake-up call for higher education and a confirmation of the damaging public perception that, too often, getting an education degree is among the easier college career paths — although it is in preparation for one of the most challenging jobs there is.[78]

In response to the easy-grading syndrome at university schools of education, NCTQ recommends:

- Teacher educators and the preparation program administrators should work together to identify common standards to define excellence. Work that is merely competent should not be awarded an A.
- Teacher educators and the preparation program should ensure that a greater proportion of assignments are "criterion-referenced," especially in early teacher-training coursework.[79]

NCTQ defines "criterion-referenced" to mean a "focus on a clearly circumscribed slice of knowledge and skill-based content, facilitating the instructors' own ability to provide substantive feedback within a defined area of expertise, as well as enabling comparisons among students as to the relative merit or quality of the completed assignments."[80]

In NCTQ's 2014 review of teacher preparation schools, the results were sobering and troubling. Among the 1,668 programs reviewed by NCTQ, only 26 elementary training programs and 81 secondary programs were able to make the list of top-ranked programs.[81]

Further, NCTQ found that "the teacher education field continues to disregard scientifically based methods of reading instruction: coursework in just 17 percent of programs equips their elementary and special education teachers to use all five fundamental components of reading instruction, helping to explain why such a large proportion of American school children (30 percent) never learn to read beyond a basic level."[82]

As for math preparation for prospective teachers, the results are just as troubling: "23 states cannot boast a single program that provides solid math preparation resembling the practices of high-performing nations."[83]

Also, "Looking across 907 undergraduate and graduate elementary programs, nearly half (47 percent) fail to ensure that teacher candidates are capable STEM instructors: these programs' requirements for candidates include little or no elementary math coursework and the programs also do not require that candidates take a single basic science course (with most giving candidates free rein to choose from a long list of narrowly focused or irrelevant electives)."[84]

The NCTQ report comes to a very sad conclusion:

> District superintendents tell us that elementary teachers simply don't know the core subjects of the elementary curriculum. We think it's no wonder that there's a "capacity gap" given the lack of guidance given to candidates about the content foundation they need before they even begin professional training.[85]

Dig deeper into teacher preparation programs and one finds that the actual textbooks used in teacher education courses are woefully deficient. A comprehensive review of teacher education textbooks by NCTQ found that "textbooks used in this coursework neglect to teach what we know about how students learn despite its central importance in training."[86] Specifically:

> Compelling cognitive research that meets scientific standards about how to teach for understanding and retention barely gets a mention in many texts, while anecdotal information is dressed up as science. Theories du jour and debunked notions are being passed on to new teachers as knowledge and best practice.[87]

There are ways, according to NCTQ, to address the deficiencies in teacher preparation programs. At university schools of education, for example, "Teacher candidates should be taught both the cognitive science that underlies the fundamental strategies of instruction and the strategies themselves in coursework that addresses instruction broadly, such as ed psych or general methods courses."[88]

At the state level, "states should first review all licensing tests that address methods of instruction to determine the research basis for those approaches."[89] Those without sufficient evidence should be removed.[90]

What all these findings show is that reforming teacher education and preparation is a monumental task and will require great and sustained effort.

RECOMMENDATIONS

- State policymakers should consult the National Council on Teacher Quality's 2016 "Learning About Learning" report to understand the depth of the problems facing teacher education and some of the possible solutions.

- While the federal government is easing up on forcing states to tie teacher preparation programs to the impact of their graduates on student outcomes, states still have the power to do so and should consider doing so.

- Thomas Arnett of the Christensen Institute says that states "need to dedicate new funding streams to disruptive innovations that fall outside the domain of accredited teacher preparation." He cites Tennessee's pilot program for coaching novice teachers and awarding them micro-credentials for demonstrating competence in particular aspects of teaching.[91]

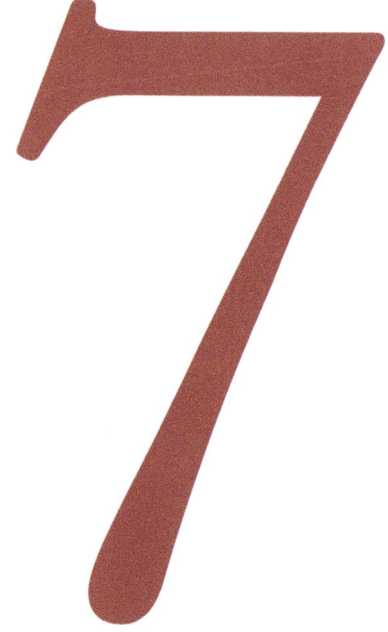

STATE AND LOCAL RECOMMENDATION

Increase Education Finance Transparency

DISCUSSION

When Congress passed the Every Students Succeeds Act (ESSA) in 2016, it included a provision requiring school districts to publish actual per-student expenditures by school on district websites. Matthew Lynch, writing in *Education Week,* observed, "This will increase transparency and help educate the public on how resources are being used."[92] However, states can do much to ensure the full implementation of the ESSA provision and to fully inform the public about where tax dollars are being spent in public education.

In California, for example, current state law requires school districts to report how they spend tax dollars, but does not require the same information for individual schools. To correct that omission, in 2017 Democrat Assemblywoman Shirley Weber of San Diego introduced legislation, AB 1321, which would require "that the reporting of per-pupil expenditures of federal, state, and local funds include actual personnel expenditures and actual non-personnel expenditures of federal, state, and local funds, as specified, for each local educational agency and school in the state, as required by a specified provision of the federal Every Student Succeeds Act."[93]

Specifically, Weber's bill would require that expenditures reported include "expenditures for administration, instruction, attendance and health services, pupil transportation services, plant operation and maintenance, fixed charges, and net expenditure to cover deficits for food services and student body activities."[94]

According to Ms. Weber, "it is time that parents, policymakers, and the public are able to clearly follow the money and ensure California's most vulnerable students are effectively served."[95]

Former California Assemblyman Ted Lempert, president of Children Now, and Ryan Smith, executive director of The Education Trust-West, write: "Parents, local communities and others should not have to hire research teams and data analysts to get the information they need to understand how school funds are being used."[96]

Even states that have good transparency programs have room to improve.

Prior to 2014, Colorado was like most states that published financial data at the school-district level rather than the individual-school level. According to the education reform organization Colorado Succeeds, "that made it impossible to gain a clear picture of where dollars actually went, and hid valuable information about which investments were providing the biggest bang for the buck."[97]

In 2014, Colorado enacted the Student Success Act, which required school-level financial transparency. As a result of that law, the Colorado Department of Education created the "Financial Transparency for Colorado Schools" website, which was unveiled in July 2017. The easy-to-navigate website provides detailed information about school finances.

According to Colorado Succeeds, which played a significant role in the passage of the Student Success Act, the law was very logically laid out:

> Under the Student Success Act, all district-run schools and public charter schools in Colorado must report financial and human resource information to the state using a standard "chart of accounts." In theory, this helps ensure that "comparable data by program and school site" appears on the financial transparency website.
>
> This requires that financial data on the state site include expenditures from every "major category" (ex: athletics, transportation) specified in the chart of accounts, and must drill down to the school level. The information on the state website must be "in a format that is readable by a layperson."

All of this is significant because if properly presented, it allows families and community members to make apples-to-apples comparison of schools within districts and among districts.

The potential benefits to parents, communities, and taxpayers are significant, helping to measure their return on investment and target additional resources toward programs that are proving successful.[98]

Colorado Succeeds notes, "the website interface is user-friendly, easy to navigate, and includes a helpful sorting function so that visitors can compare up to four schools at one time." Further, "It includes salary and benefit expenditures by job category, shedding light on important costs associated with school personnel."[99]

However, the group points out that despite the requirement that spending in every major category must be reported at the school level, "some districts have chosen not to assign expenditures for categories such as transportation, athletics, centralized services, and food service operations to their individual schools."[100]

In addition, Coloradans could be confused by the fact "that because certain school districts decided to account for some expenditures only at the centralized level, district per-pupil spending figures are much higher than those figures for individual schools."[101]

Finally, says the group, "even within districts, individual school reporting is inconsistent," which "creates confusion and distorts true spending levels and allocation."[102]

Colorado Succeeds warns: "If Coloradans using the financial transparency website cannot make apple-to-apple comparisons, this tool, which has such great potential to help school leaders identify and implement best practices from other high-performing schools, becomes far less useful."

There is a lot that states and local school districts can do to improve the transparency of education finances. Good model legislation, such as the American Legislative Exchange Council's excellent "Public School Financial Transparency Act" are available, and good first attempts like Colorado's Student Success Act can be studied.

In the end, however, it is imperative for the public and parents to be informed about how their tax dollars are being spent so that they can make critical judgments on the functioning of their public school systems and the need for reform.

RECOMMENDATIONS

- States and districts need to take stock of their current education finance reporting to the public.

- States and school districts should look at transparency models such as Colorado's program, noting both the positives and deficiencies of those transparency efforts, and model legislation created by ALEC and others.

STATE AND LOCAL RECOMMENDATION

8 Create Strong Accountability Plans Under The Every Student Succeeds Act

DISCUSSION

Ever since the federal No Child Left Behind Act was passed in 2001, states have had to come up with accountability plans and programs. Now under the Every Student Succeeds Act states will once again have to produce accountability plans.

The rationale underlying ESSA is that states and local education agencies will have greater control and autonomy than under NCLB. As states take advantage of that autonomy in their designing of accountability plans, the Fordham Institute makes a couple of common-sense recommendations:

- **Intuitive Ratings.** For more than two decades now, school ratings have been at the heart of state accountability systems—and for good reason. Easy-to-understand labels, such as A–F letter grades, provide clear signals to parents, citizens, and educators about the quality of a school and can nudge systems toward improvement. "Dashboards of data" are great complements to this, especially when teams sit down to determine how to take a school to the next level, but they are no replacement. Furthermore, there's simply no excuse for states to assign labels that are impossible to parse, which strikes us as an Orwellian approach to keep interested parties in the dark about school quality.

- **A Focus on All Students.** We understand the impulse to make low-performing students a priority. Many U.S. schools need to do far better by them, and before NCLB, their needs were often ignored. But they aren't the only children who matter, and acting as if they are signals to schools that students who are already proficient don't deserve to have their education maximized. Such neglect is inequitable. It's also bad for social mobility and harmful to the country's long-term prosperity. [103]

As states decide the particulars of their accountability plans, policymakers should also look at thoughtful critiques and responses such as a detailed 2017 letter analyzing the Colorado draft ESSA accountability plan signed by a diverse coalition of 24 groups including A+ Colorado, Education Reform Now, Democrats for Education Reform, Colorado Succeeds, the NAACP and Latino organizations.[104]

Writing in the *Education Post*, Lisa Berdie, policy director at A+ Colorado, says that the state accountability plan overly relies on non-goal-focused measurements: "each of the components of Colorado accountability . . . is a normative measure—a measure that tells us how students, schools and districts perform relative to other students, schools and districts. What we miss with normative measures is the chance to understand whether or not students are mastering particular content or skills, which is what we get when we use criterion-based measures."[105]

According to the education publication *The 74*, an independent review of the 17 state accountability plans submitted to the U.S. Department of Education as part of the ESSA requirements "cautioned that state plans are turning to a 'normative-based accountability' system—that is, how well schools are doing in relation to one another, rather than against a set benchmark."[106]

For example, "Massachusetts's plan would measure growth by comparing students to one another rather than an objective standard, and growth and proficiency standards aren't aligned to grade-level standards, the reviewers said," and the plan "lacks specifics on how low-performing schools will be identified."[107]

"In Colorado," Lisa Berdie explains, "I can tell you which schools are moving the ball down the field (growth), but I can't tell you how close they are to a touchdown or even how many yards they have moved (i.e. proficiency)."[108]

"Previously, Colorado's accountability system *did* incorporate measures that actually communicated to communities whether or not students were meeting the expectations that would set them up for college or career success," but, she laments, "Not so anymore."[109]

The letter signed by Berdie's group and the 23 other organizations has well-reasoned arguments on a whole array of accountability issues. The goal of the signers is accountability for the achievement of every student. While not everyone would agree with every one of their recommendations, their thoughtful consideration of everything from testing metrics to school interventions to English–language learners to easily accessible and user-friendly data to robust community engagement is worth pondering by policymakers, not only in Colorado, but in other states as well.

RECOMMENDATION

- States should look to recommendations of the Fordham Institute and the Colorado coalition (cited above) as they seek to strengthen their ESSA-required accountability plans.

STATE AND LOCAL RECOMMENDATION

Improve School Safety (repeal and replace anti-suspension policies)

DISCUSSION

According to a 2016 report by the U.S. Department of Education and the U.S. Department of Justice, during the 2013-14 school year, an amazing 65 percent of public schools reported that one or more incidents of violence had taken place, which translated into an estimated 757,000 crimes.

As mentioned earlier, in the face of this wave of violence on school campuses, the federal government under President Obama pushed states and local school districts to adopt more lenient suspension and discipline policies. However, many states and districts have been happy to adopt such policies, regardless of any push from Washington.

Twenty-seven states have enacted laws that have limited the use of suspensions and other so-called "exclusionary discipline policies." A 2017 study on school discipline by the New York-based Manhattan Institute notes:

> The most sweeping . . . was California's law that imposed stricter limits on the use of suspensions for nonviolent "willful defiance" offenses. Illinois passed a law that prohibited districts from using "zero-tolerance" discipline policies and encouraged them to exhaust other options before issuing a suspension. In Georgia, students have a right to a disciplinary hearing before being suspended . . . .[110]

In addition, the Manhattan Institute study found 53 of America's largest school districts, covering more than 6.3 million students, have revised their discipline codes to reduce the use of suspensions.[111]

At the extreme, the Los Angeles Unified School District has virtually banned suspensions, with the rate falling to near zero percent.[112]

In 2015, New York City mayor Bill de Blasio implemented new requirements on the city's public schools making it much more difficult to suspend disruptive students. Analyzing data from the New York City school-climate survey, a Manhattan Institute study found that from 2013-14 to 2015-16, "more than half of schools saw a deterioration in mutual respect, and only a fifth saw an improvement, according to students." Further, "On physical fighting, gang activity, and drug use, three times as many schools saw a deterioration as saw an improvement, according to students."[113]

It must be emphasized that this deterioration is according to the students, who must interact with their peers, including the disruptive ones, all throughout the school day. In terms of the number of public schools where things had deteriorated:

> In 2015-16, for example, there were 154 more schools than in 2013-14 where more than half of students said that students did not respect one another (387 vs. 243); there were 46 more schools where 30+% of students reported frequent gang activity; there were 32 more schools where 30+% of students reported frequent drug/alcohol use; there were 105 more schools where 30+% of students reported frequent physical fights; and there were 28 more schools where 30+% of teachers said that order and discipline were not maintained.[114]

Schools especially hard hit by de Blasio's anti-suspensions policies are those with high minority student populations: "According to students, schools that serve 90+% minority students saw the most significant deterioration in school climate under the de Blasio discipline reform – compared with schools serving a lower percentage of minority students." For example, fighting increased in half of the schools with high minority populations and mutual respect deteriorated in 58 percent of the high-minority schools.[115]

In 2015-16, New York City Public Schools meted out nearly 16,000 fewer suspensions than in 2013-14, with the result that more than 375,000 students attended a school "where a higher percentage of teachers reported that order and discipline were not maintained."[116]

The Manhattan Institute study concludes: "But standardized test scores are, fundamentally, a second-order concern." More important to parents and their children, "If we believe what students and teachers report, hundreds of thousands of students in New York City are now being educated in schools that are less respectful, less orderly, and more violent."[117] In view of these findings, "what we know now should alarm parents – and not only those in New York."[118]

The disturbing impact of such policy outcomes cannot be overstated. Thus, there is evidence that disruptive students left in the classroom have a significantly negative effect on the learning of their fellow students. According to a study by researchers at the University of California at Davis and the University of Pittsburgh:

> Our results indicate that troubled students have a statistically significant negative effect on their peers' reading and math test scores. Adding one troubled student to a classroom of 20 students results in a decrease in student reading and math test scores of more than two-thirds of a percentile point (2 to 3 percent of a standard deviation).[119]

In addition, a single disruptive student "also significantly increases misbehavior of other students in the classroom," causing them to commit 16 percent more infractions than they otherwise would. The researchers also found that disruptive student behavior had an especially negative impact on higher-income children's math and reading achievement, and on the misbehavior of low-income children.[120]

Perhaps the most cautionary finding that the researchers discovered was the impact of disruptive behavior by boys on other boys:

> Across all outcome variables, both academic and behavioral, the negative peer effects appear to be driven primarily by the troubled boys, and these effects are largest on other boys in the classroom. The results indicate that adding one troubled boy to a classroom of 20 students decreases boys' test scores by nearly 2 percentile points (7 percent of a standard deviation) and increases the probability that a boy will commit a disciplinary infraction by 4.4 percentile points (17 percent). Apparently, troubled boys generate the strongest adverse peer effects, and other boys are most sensitive to their influence.[121]

The researchers conclude that their findings "provide strong evidence of the validity of the 'bad apple' peer effects model, which hypothesizes that a single disruptive student can negatively affect the outcomes for all other students in the classroom."[122]

Some schools, fed up with student behavior problems, are returning to tough suspension policies.

In 2016-17 at Harrisburg High School in Pennsylvania, 500 students have been given suspension notices for skipping at least a week's work of classes. Principal Lisa Love said that students often go to school but then skip class and loiter in hallways and other parts of the school.

"If you're not in class," said Love, "all you're here to do then is to wreak havoc upon the school and disrupt the work that we are trying to do here." Love says that the student class-skippers disrupt the school's "focus on student achievement."[123]

"We don't like to suspend," Love emphasized, but "we need to send the message that the value of education comes first." Her supportive school superintendent, Sybill Knight-Burney, said that the school's decision should serve as a "wake-up call" to the community.[124]

"In order for us to get different results, we have to do something different," said the superintendent, and, "We can't be doing the same old, same old, and complain when we're getting the same results."[125]

Principal Love and Superintendent Knight-Burney are ultimately protecting the interests of those students who want to go to school and go to class and learn. Sadly, however the thinking and policies of Love and Knight-Burney are going against the overwhelming anti-suspension, anti-discipline tide in the nation's public schools.

Writing in the publication *City Journal*, Manhattan Institute senior fellow Heather Mac Donald said: "Protecting well-behaved students' ability to learn is a school's highest obligation, and it is destroyed when teachers lose the option of removing chronically disruptive students from class."[126]

RECOMMENDATIONS:

- States and local school districts should repeal anti-suspension laws and policies that endanger the safety of students and school personnel.
- States and local school districts should adopt laws and policies that guarantee significant consequences for misbehavior, disruption, violence and criminal activity by students, and protect the safety of all innocent students.

10 Expand Teacher Choice

STATE AND LOCAL RECOMMENDATION

DISCUSSION

The choice movement in education is not just about empowering parents and their children to choose the best schooling option to meet their needs. It is also about giving teachers freedom of choice when it comes to their employment, especially the freedom to choose whether they want teacher unions to take part of their earnings and represent them in contract negotiations. This critical issue was at the heart of the *Friedrichs v. California Teachers Association* case that went before the United States Supreme Court in 2016.

The non-union teacher plaintiffs in the *Friedrichs* case argued that union-bargained contracts, which cover both union and non-union teachers, are inherently political documents and often contain policies detrimental to teachers and students, such as uniform salaries, inflexible tenure rules and lax discipline standards. According to the plaintiffs, forcing them to pay so-called "agency shop" fees to the unions to negotiate such contracts violated their First Amendment rights of free speech and free association. Key justices agreed.

"The problem," posited Justice Antonin Scalia, "is that everything that is collectively bargained with the government is within the political sphere, almost by definition."[127]

"Should the government pay higher wages or lesser wages," queried Scalia, or "should it promote teachers on the basis of seniority." He observed, "All of those questions are necessarily political questions."[128]

The court was therefore on the brink of ruling that workers could not be forced to fund public employee unions, among the most powerful organizations in America. Such a decision would have had earth-shattering political and policy consequences. Yet, it turned out not to be.

In the wake of conservative Justice Antonin Scalia's death, the U.S. Supreme Court delivered a 4-4 tie vote in the *Friedrichs* case, which meant that a Ninth Circuit ruling against the non-union plaintiffs will hold sway for the time being.

A similar case, *Janus v. AFSCME*, may give the Supreme Court, and new justice Neil Gorsuch, a second chance to decide the issues that came before it in the *Friedrichs* case. However, regardless of the Supreme Court's ultimate actions, there are things that states can do now to ensure teachers' freedom of speech and association.

For example, in 2011, Wisconsin enacted Act 10, which among other things, stopped requiring teachers to pay dues to the teachers union. States should at least enact laws that allow non-union teachers to be free to choose whether they want to pay agency fees to the teacher unions for collective-bargaining purposes.

Nearly half of the states still force non-union teachers to pay agency fees to teacher unions.

As Rebecca Friedrichs, the teacher-plaintiff in the Supreme Court case said, "I hope that teachers, and other public-sector workers will be free to decide for themselves, without fear or coercion, whether or not to join or fund a union."[129]

RECOMMENDATION

- States should adopt laws that prevent teacher unions from requiring teachers to pay dues to a union or to pay agency fees for collective bargaining.

ENDNOTES

1. Eric Boehm, "End the Ed? Rep. Massie Says Department of Education's Days Could Be Numbered, Reason.com, " April 26, 2017, available at http://reason.com/blog/2017/04/26/end-the-ed-rep-massie-says-department-of
2. Alexander Holt, "How Trump Could Abolish the Department of Education," New America, February 15, 2017, available at https://www.newamerica.org/education-policy/edcentral/how-trump-could-abolish-department-education/
3. Ibid.
4. Ibid.
5. Ibid.
6. Bruce Meredith and Mark Paige, "For better schools, abolish the politicized Department of Education and give local districts more control," *Los Angeles Times*, January 7, 2017, available at http://www.latimes.com/opinion/op-ed/la-oe-meredith-paige-abolish-education-department-20170106-story.html
7. "Trump orders study of federal role in education," *The Washington Post*, April 26, 2017, available at https://www.washingtonpost.com/local/education/trump-expected-to-order-study-of-federal-role-in-education/2017/04/26/577dddbc-2a19-11e7-a616-d7c8a68c1a66_story.html?utm_term=.b5f7c1d2d483
8. Ibid.
9. See, for example, President Reagan's 1984 State of the Union, where he cited the Grace Commission report and recommendations, available at https://www.youtube.com/watch?v=TdMTTlpfNP4
10. Larry Mone, ""A tax credit is a great way to fulfill Trump's pledge on school choice," *New York Post*, May 18, 2017, available at http://nypost.com/2017/05/18/a-tax-credit-is-a-great-way-to-fulfill-trumps-pledge-on-school-choice/

11   "AFC Urges Federal Action to Expand Educational Opportunity in America," American Federation of Children, February 22, 2017, available at https://www.federationforchildren.org/federal-action/

12   Larry Mone, ""A tax credit is a great way to fulfill Trump's pledge on school choice," *New York Post*, May 18, 2017, available at http://nypost.com/2017/05/18/a-tax-credit-is-a-great-way-to-fulfill-trumps-pledge-on-school choice/

13   Nat Malkus, "A diversified approach to federal investment in school choice in a bull market," American Enterprise Institute, March 10, 2017, available at http://www.aei.org/publication/a-diversified-approach-to-federal-investment-in-school choice-in-a-bull-market/

14   Ibid.

15   Ibid.

16   Thomas Carroll, "A 50-state scholarship tax credit," Fordham Institute, February 27, 2017, available at https://edexcellence.net/articles/a-50-state-scholarship-tax-credit

17   "AFC Urges Federal Action to Expand Educational Opportunity in America," American Federation of Children, February 22, 2017, available at https://www.federationforchildren.org/federal-action/

18   Ibid.

19   Ibid.

20   "Joint 'Dear Colleague Letter,'" U.S. Department of Justice Civil Rights Division and U.S. Department of Education Office of Civil Rights, January 8, 2014, available at https://www2.ed.gov/about/offices/list/ocr/letters/colleague-201401-title-vi.html

21   Ibid.

22   Max Eden, "School Discipline Reform and Disorder: Evidence from New York City Public Schools, 2012-16," Manhattan Institute, March 2017, p. 8, available at https://www.manhattan-institute.org/sites/default/files/R-ME-0217.pdf

23   John Paul Wright, et al, "Prior problem behavior accounts for the racial gap in school suspensions," *Journal of Criminal Justice*, 2014, available at https://c8.nrostatic.com/sites/default/files/pdf_article_040214_KC_HeatherMac.pdf

24   Ibid.

25   Ibid.

26   Ibid.

27   Scott Carrell and Mark Hoekstra, "Domino Effect," *EducationNext*, Summer 2009, Vol. 9, No. 3, available at http://educationnext.org/domino-effect-2/

28   Ibid.
29   Ibid.
30   Elizabeth Mann, "The prospects of DeVos' school choice agenda as Ed Secretary," *Brown Center Chalkboard*, Brookings Institution, November 29, 2016, available at https://www.brookings.edu/blog/brown-center-chalkboard/2016/11/29/the-prospects-of-devoss-school choice-agenda-as-ed-secretary/?utm_campaign=Brookings+Brief&utm_source=hs_email&utm_medium=email&utm_content=38416034
31   Ibid.
32   "Transcript of Education Secretary DeVos' Interview with AP," Associated Press, August 14, 2017, available at https://www.apnews.com/f464361c-49544ce4b812acdcbbd9efff/Transcript-of-Education-Secretary-DeVos%27-Interview-with-AP
33   Marion Smith, "100 Years of Communism's Bloody History," *The Daily Beast*, April 22, 2017, available at http://www.thedailybeast.com/100-years-of-communisms-bloody-legacy
34   Ibid.
35   Peggy Carr, "2015 National Assessment of Educational Progress (NAEP) Grades 4 and 8 Mathematics and Reading," National Center for Education Statistics, October 28, 2015, available at https://nces.ed.gov/WhatsNew/commissioner/remarks2015/10_28_2015.asp
36   Ibid.
37   "Math Scores Drop for 4th and 8th Grades," *Education Week*, October 28, 2015, available at http://blogs.edweek.org/edweek/curriculum/2015/10/math_naep_scores_drop_for_4th_8th_grades.html?cmp=eml-enl-eu-news2
38   Susan Berry, "Student Performance Declines on National Tests Following Common Core Implementation," *Breitbart News*, October 28, 2015, available at http://www.breitbart.com/big-government/2015/10/28/student-performance-declines-national-tests-following-common-core-implementation/
39   Ibid.
40   Math Scores Drop for 4th and 8th Grades," *Education Week*, October 28, 2015, available at http://blogs.edweek.org/edweek/curriculum/2015/10/math_naep_scores_drop_for_4th_8th_grades.html?cmp=eml-enl-eu-news2
41   Susan Berry, "Edu Sec'y: Test Scores Embarassing Because Schools 'Retooling' to Common Core," *Breitbart News*, April 28, 2016, available at http://www.breitbart.com/big-government/2016/04/28/edu-secy-test-scores-embarrassing-because-schools-retooling-to-common-core/
42   Ibid.
43   Blake Neef, "Has Common Core Just Been Repealed? These Senators Think So," *The Daily Caller*, December 11, 2015, available at http://dailycaller.com/2015/12/11/no-the-new-education-law-doesnt-repeal-common-core/

44 Ibid.
45 Ibid.
46 See Sandra Stotsky, "How Massachusetts Promoted Achievement Before Common Core and PARCC," Pioneer Institute, August 18, 2015, available at http://pioneerinstitute.org/education/how-massachusetts-promoted-achievement-before-common-core-parcc/
47 Leona Christy, et al, "Student Achievement in Charter Schools: What the Research Shows," National Charter School Resource Center, 2015, p. 20, available at https://www.charterschoolcenter.org/sites/default/files/files/field_publication_attachment/Student%20Achievement%20in%20Charter%20Schools_0.pdf
48 Sarah Cordes, "In Pursuit of the Common Good: Spillover Effects of Charter Schools on Public School Students in New York City," Temple University, 2017, available at https://drive.google.com/file/d/0BxrKdaoARx08Y19ZdEF5emhxbTQ/view
49 "Measuring Up to the Model: Rankings of State Charter School Laws," National Alliance of Public Charter Schools, January 2016, p. 8, available at http://www.publiccharters.org/wp-content/uploads/2016/01/Model-Law-Final_2016.pdf?x87663
50 Ibid., p. 50.
51 Ibid., p. 51.
52 Ibid., p. 40.
53 Greg Forster, "A Win-Win Solution: The Empirical Evidence for School Choice," *EdChoice*, May 2016, p. 1, available at http://www.edchoice.org/wp-content/uploads/2016/05/2016-5-Win-Win-Solution-WEB.pdf
54 Patrick Wolf, et al, "The Participant Effects of Private School Vouchers across the Globe: A Meta-Analytic and Systemic Review," University of Arkansas Department of Education Reform, May 10, 2016, EDRE Working Paper 2016-07, p. 40, available at http://www.uaedreform.org/downloads/2016/05/the-participant-effects-of-private-school-vouchers-across-the-globe-a-meta-analytic-and-systematic-review-2.pdf
55 Lance Izumi, *The Corrupt Classroom: Bias, Indoctrination, Violence, and Social Engineering Show Why America Needs School Choice* (San Francisco, CA: Pacific Research Institute, 2017).
56 Martin West, et al, "The 2017 EdNext Poll on School Reform," *EducationNext*, Winter 2018, Vol. 18, No. 1, available at http://educationnext.org/2017-ednext-poll-school-reform-public-opinion-school choice-common-core-higher-ed/
57 "Most Favor Vouchers, Yet Most Give Local Schools Good Grades," Public Policy Institute of California, April 19, 2017, available at http://www.ppic.org/press-release/most-favor-vouchers-yet-most-give-local-schools-good-grades/
58 Ibid.
59 Ibid.

60 Lance Izumi, "Powerful testimony in trial on tenure," *Orange County Register*, February 10, 2014, available at http://www.ocregister.com/2014/02/10/lance-t-izumi-powerful-testimony-in-trial-on-tenure/
61 Ibid.
62 Ibid.
63 Ibid.
64 Ibid.
65 Ibid.
66 Ibid.
67 Lance Izumi, "*Vergara* Decision: Remember the Children the Court Forgot," *Fox & Hounds*, May 16, 2016, available at http://www.foxandhoundsdaily.com/2016/05/vergara-decision-remember-children-court-forgot/
68 Michael Horn, "Finding 'personalized learning' and other edtech buzzwords on the Gartner Hype Cycle," Christensen Institute, January 19, 2017, available at https://www.christenseninstitute.org/blog/finding-personalized-learning-edtech-buzzwords-gartner-hype-cycle/
69 Esther Wojcicki and Lance Izumi, *Moonshots in Education* (San Francisco, CA: Pacific Research Institute, 2015), p. 216.
70 "State Strategies for Awarding Credit to Support Student Learning," National Governors Association Issue Brief, February 1, 2012, p. 3, available at https://www.nga.org/cms/home/nga-center-for-best-practices/center-publications/page-edu-publications/col2-content/main-content-list/state-strategies-for-awarding-cr.html
71 Ibid.
72 "Create Personalized, Competency-Based Education Systems," International Association for K-12 Learning (iNACOL), available at https://www.inacol.org/our-work/inacol-center-for-policy-advocacy/
73 June Ahn, "Enrollment and Achievement in Ohio's Virtual Charter Schools," Fordham Institute, August 2, 2016, p. 5, available at http://edex.s3-us-west-2.amazonaws.com/publication/pdfs/%2808.02%29%20Enrollment%20and%20Achievement%20in%20Ohio%27s%20Virtual%20Charter%20Schools.pdf
74 Ibid., see p. 6.
75 Michael Horn, ""Harnessing benefits, reining in downsides of virtual schools," *Forbes*, August 25, 2016, available at https://www.forbes.com/sites/michaelhorn/2016/08/25/harnessing-benefits-reigning-in-downsides-of-virtual-schools/2/#3f9853451c17
76 Ibid.
77 "Disconnected and Unaccountable Teacher Training is at the Heart of Schooling Failure," Education Consumers Federation, available at http://education-consumers.org/teacher-prep/
78 "Easy A's," National Council for Teacher Quality, pp. 1-2, available at http://nctq.org/dmsView/Easy_As_exec_summary
79 Ibid.

80 Ibid.
81 "NCTQ Teacher Prep Review 2014," National Council for Teacher Quality, 2014, p. 2, available at http://www.nctq.org/dmsView/Teacher_Prep_Review_2014_executive_summary
82 Ibid., p. 3.
83 Ibid.
84 Ibid.
85 Ibid.
86 "Learning About Learning: What Every Teacher Needs to Know," National Council on Teacher Quality, January 2016, p. v, available at http://www.nctq.org/dmsView/Learning_About_Learning_Report
87 Ibid.
88 Ibid., p. 28.
89 Ibid., p. 29.
90 Ibid.
91 Thomas Arnett, "Will Trump's deregulation help teacher preparation," *EducationNext*, April 12, 2017, available at http://educationnext.org/will-trumps-deregulation-help-teacher-preparation/
92 Matthey Lynch, "Is Your District Ready for Financial Transparency?," *Education Week*, March 6, 2017, available at http://blogs.edweek.org/edweek/education_futures/2017/03/is_your_district_ready_for_financial_transparency.html
93 See AB 1321 at https://leginfo.legislature.ca.gov/faces/billNavClient.xhtml?bill_id=201720180AB1321
94 Ibid.
95 "Bill to Help the Parents, Policymakers, and Public Follow the Money Will Be Referred to Assembly Education Committee," April 3, 2017, available at https://a79.asmdc.org/press-releases/bill-help-parents-policymakers-and-public-follow-money-will-be-referred-assembly
96 Ted Lempert and Ryan Smith, "My Word: Transparency desperately needed on school funding," *East Bay Times*, April 16, 2017, available at http://www.eastbaytimes.com/2017/04/16/my-word-transparency-desperately-needed-on-school-funding/
97 "Colorado Leads the Way on School Financial Transparency—But There's Still Room to Grow," Colorado Succeeds, August 2, 2017, available at http://www.coloradosucceeds.org/blog/colorado-leads-the-way-on-school-financial-transparency-still-room-to-grow/
98 Ibid.
99 Ibid.
100 Ibid.
101 Ibid.

102 Ibid.
103 Randall Wright and Michael Petrilli, "Rating the Ratings: Analyzing the First 17 ESSA Accountability Plans," Fordham Institute, July 27, 2017, pp. 6-7, available at http://edex.s3-us-west-2.amazonaws.com/publication/pdfs/%2807.27%29%20Rating%20the%20Ratings%20-%20Analyzing%20the%20First%2017%20ESSA%20Accountability%20Plans.pdf
104 Letter to Commissioner Kathy Anthens," March 13, 2017, available at http://apluscolorado.org/wp-content/uploads/2017/03/ESSAplan.CoalitionResponse.FINAL_.pdf
105 Lisa Berdie, "Colorado's ESSA Plan Doesn't Quite Get All Students Across the Goal Line," *Education Post*, April 14, 2017, available at http://educationpost.org/colorados-essa-plan-doesnt-quite-get-all-kids-across-the-goal-line/
106 "Independent Review of ESSA Plans Rates States Strong on Accountability, Weak on Counting All Kids," *The 74*, June 26, 2017, available at https://www.the74million.org/article/exclusive-independent-review-of-essa-plans-rates-states-strong-on-accountability-weak-on-counting-all-kids
107 Ibid.
108 Lisa Berdie, "Colorado's ESSA Plan Doesn't Quite Get All Students Across the Goal Line," *Education Post*, April 14, 2017, available at http://educationpost.org/colorados-essa-plan-doesnt-quite-get-all-kids-across-the-goal-line/
109 Ibid.
110 Max Eden, "School Discipline Reform and Disorder: Evidence from New York City Public Schools, 2012-16," Manhattan Institute, March 2017, p. 9, available at https://www.manhattan-institute.org/sites/default/files/R-ME-0217.pdf
111 Ibid, p. 8.
112 Ibid.
113 Ibid., p. 17.
114 Ibid, p. 18.
115 Ibid, pp. 21-22.
116 Ibid, p. 24.
117 Ibid.
118 Ibid, p. 25.
119 Scott Carrell and Mark Hoekstra, "Domino Effect," *EducationNext*, Summer 2009, Vol. 9, No. 3, available at http://educationnext.org/domino-effect-2/
120 Ibid.
121 Ibid.

122 Ibid.
123 "Pennsylvania high school gives nearly 500 students suspension notices," FoxNews.com, March 31, 2017, available at http://www.foxnews.com/us/2017/03/31/pennsylvania-high-school-gives-nearly-500-students-suspension-notices.html
124 Ibid.
125 Ibid.
126 Heather Mac Donald, "Undisciplined: The Obama Administration Undermines Classroom Order in Pursuit of Phantom Racism," *City Journal*, Sumer 2012, available at https://www.city-journal.org/html/undisciplined-13485.html
127 Lance Izumi, "The Friedrichs Case: Why the Supreme Court pick means so much," *The Hill*, August 15, 2016, available at http://thehill.com/blogs/congress-blog/judicial/291457-the-friedrichs-case-why-the-supreme-court-pick-means-so-much
128 Ibid.
129 Lance Izumi, "Friedrichs decision isn't end in fight against public-sector unions," *Washington Examiner*, April 9, 2016, available at http://www.washingtonexaminer.com/friedrichs-decision-isnt-end-in-fight-against-public-sector-unions/article/2588052

ABOUT THE AUTHOR

LANCE T. IZUMI, J.D.

Lance Izumi is Koret Senior Fellow in Education Studies and Senior Director of the Center for Education at the Pacific Research Institute, a public policy think tank based in San Francisco, Sacramento, and Pasadena, California. He is the author of numerous books, including his most recent, *The Corrupt Classroom*. He has authored many studies and articles on education policy issues, and served as co-executive producer of an award-winning PBS-broadcast documentary on underperforming middle-class public schools and co-executive producer, writer and narrator of a *New York Times*-posted short film on school choice.

In 2016-17, Lance served on President Trump's transition Agency Action Team for education policy.

From 2004 to 2015, he served as a member of the Board of Governors of the California Community Colleges, the largest system of higher education in the nation, and served two terms as president of the Board from 2008 to 2009.

In 2015, he was elected chair of the board of directors of the Foundation for California Community Colleges, the official non-profit that supports the community college system and the state Chancellor's Office.

He also served as a commissioner on the California Postsecondary Education Commission and as a member of the United States Civil Rights Commission's California Advisory Committee.

Previously, he served as chief speechwriter and director of writing and research for California Governor George Deukmejian and as speechwriter to United States Attorney General Edwin Meese III in President Ronald Reagan's administration.

Lance received his juris doctorate from the University of Southern California School of Law, his master of arts in political science from the University of California at Davis, and his bachelor of arts in economics and history from the University of California at Los Angeles.

ABOUT PRI

The Pacific Research Institute (PRI) champions freedom, opportunity, and personal responsibility by advancing free-market policy solutions. It provides practical solutions for the policy issues that impact the daily lives of all Americans, and demonstrates why the free market is more effective than the government at providing the important results we all seek: good schools, quality health care, a clean environment, and a robust economy.

Founded in 1979 and based in San Francisco, PRI is a non-profit, non-partisan organization supported by private contributions. Its activities include publications, public events, media commentary, community leadership, legislative testimony, and academic outreach.

Business and Economic Studies
PRI shows how the entrepreneurial spirit—the engine of economic growth and opportunity—is stifled by onerous taxes, regulations, and lawsuits. It advances policy reforms that promote a robust economy, consumer choice, and innovation.

Education Studies
PRI works to restore to all parents the basic right to choose the best educational opportunities for their children. Through research and grassroots outreach, PRI promotes parental choice in education, high academic standards, teacher quality, charter schools, and school-finance reform.

Environmental Studies
PRI reveals the dramatic and long-term trend toward a cleaner, healthier environment. It also examines and promotes the essential ingredients for abundant resources and environmental quality: property rights, markets, local action, and private initiative.

Health Care Studies
PRI demonstrates why a single-payer Canadian model would be detrimental to the health care of all Americans. It proposes market-based reforms that would improve affordability, access, quality, and consumer choice.

Center for California Reform
The Center for California Reform seeks to reinvigorate California's entrepreneurial self-reliant traditions. It champions solutions in education, business, and the environment that work to advance prosperity and opportunity for all the state's residents.

www.ingramcontent.com/pod-product-compliance
Lightning Source LLC
Chambersburg PA
CBHW051334110526
44591CB00026B/2994